Side Hustles

B. Vincent

Published by RWG Publishing, 2021.

SIDE HUSTLES

First edition. August 13, 2021.

Written by B. Vincent.

Also by B. Vincent

Bookkeeping
Bridge Pages
Business Acquisition
Business Bogging
Marketing Automation
Better Meetings
Conversion Optimization
Creative Solutions
Employee Recruitment
Startup Capital
Employee Mentoring
Followership
Servant Leadership
Human Resources
Team Building
Freelancing
Funnel Building
Geo Targeting
Goal Setting
Immanent List Building
Lead Generation
Leadership Course
Leadership Transition
LinkedIn Ads
LinkedIn Marketing
Messenger Marketing
New Management
Newsfeed Ads
Search Ads
Online Learning
Sales Webinars

Side Hustles

Table of Contents

Side Hustles

Welcome to this seminar on side hustles. In this course, we will cover how to expand your pay. By tracking down a side gig, this course is isolated into three modules. Module. One gives you a concise introduction to the side hustle idea. Module two goes over some online side hustle thoughts and module three covers some disconnected alternatives for side hustles. When this course is finished. You'll realize how to help your pay with a side hustle that works for you. So, moving along, how about we jump into the principal module. OK folks, welcome to module one. In this module, our master will give you a short introduction to side hustles. So, prepare to take a few notes and we should directly bounce in.

Module One

Module one, introduction to side hustles. On the off chance that he needs to acquire an excess to have a side hustle, a side hustle is basically characterized as an additional work. Notwithstanding your normal everyday employment side hustles turn out strengthening revenue for the individuals who are hoping to bring shortly more money, or for the individuals who are hoping to get by as monetary security keeps on being an issue. Overall side hustles are essential for the individuals who need to escape obligation. It can even in the long run become a venturing stone for entering the enterprising scene. Assuming you need to become familiar with how to bring in cash as an afterthought, then, at that point this is the aide for you. Part one spotlights on the advantages you can get from having an additional pay. Part two gives you a rundown of online side gigs that you can do. At long last, section three, examines choices for disconnected side hustles.

When you're done perusing this course, you're presently prepared to assume the universe of side hustling. As per bank rate side hustle overview in 2019 45% of working Americans around 70 million have a gig outside their normal everyday employment. At the point when asked the justification what valid reason they're doing it. 30% said that they need the additional cash to earn a living wage. Besides, generally 60% said that they utilize the cash principally for investment funds or as discretionary cashflow for spending. Here are some additional amazing measurements. An individual spends a normal of 11 to 16 hours out of every week doing side hustles side hustles have a normal hourly pace of $16 to $23 60 minutes. 27% of side tricksters began bringing in cash from a side interest. 1% of the American labor force utilize an application-based stage to acquire pay. 47% of individuals with post-graduate have decided on side hustles. 48% of twenty-to-thirty-year old's have a side hustle.

30% of side tricksters are through exchanging or selling carefully assembled items. 54% of side tricksters are ladies. These insights show how side hustles are evolving. The manner in which we take a gander at acquiring more pay, regardless of whether it's for a reasonable or individual reason side hustles can help you not exclusively to procure more, however, to help you take a stab at something new, particularly in case you're thinking about a lifelong change. Truth be told, some even viewed as a side hustle as a type of pastime. Then again, individuals procuring through these gigs understand that they can earn enough to pay the rent while not completely depending on the customary work models. As the idea of work developed through time side hustles have revealed insight into the possibility that individuals can have the chance to transform work into a pastime. In case you're somebody who's hoping to begin on having side gigs, your inspiration might originate from either monetary or imaginative reasons, whatever your expectation is.

Here are three reasons why you ought to have a side hustle turns out additional revenue. Having a thought extra stream of pay can be useful on some random day, regardless of whether it's to take care of your obligations, support reserve funds, fabricate your abundance quicker, or just having additional money to treat yourself sometimes. Having an additional pay likewise implies that you're not completely dependent on your normal everyday employment. Losing your regular employment can be truly distressing, particularly when you're living check to check. Nonetheless, side hustles fill in as pads that give you a touch of extra monetary abilities immaculateness. It tends to enable having indeed, side hustle assists you with bringing in additional money, yet additionally adds to your general government assistance. As you begin bringing in cash from close to, you'll acquire new abilities or work on existing ones, discovering gigs that you have a genuine premium in lights your energy that you in any case may lose.

On the off chance that you exclusively centered around your customary work, also side hustles engage you, realizing that you have a financial worth outside of your everyday work, this sensation of satisfaction and empowers you to have a superior way of life and appreciate life without limit. Not taking a very remarkable danger. Numerous entrepreneurs have made a major, unnerving jump when they chose to leave their regular positions and seek after their fantasy about building their own business. In any case, with that large of a danger, this can't be feasible for everybody. Notwithstanding, with a side hustle, you can begin chipping away at a business without losing the security of your primary kind of revenue. This likewise implies that it'd be to a lesser degree a weight to change plans. In case things aren't working out, you can zero in additional on your enthusiasm. There are innumerable accounts of individuals who have transformed their enthusiasm into something productive. You too can do likewise. Indeed, you may wind up transforming your enthusiasm into a task that you'll really cherish. For example, innovative personalities have transformed their thoughts into concrete, unmistakable items that they sell on the web. Meanwhile partaking in the creative cycle, bringing in cash is only one of the advantages of accomplishing something you genuinely appreciate.

Module Two

Hello people, welcome to module two. In this module, our master will go over some online side hustle thoughts. So, prepare to take a few notes and how about we hop directly in

Module two online side hustle thoughts as the progression of innovation improves and the web turns into a fundamental piece of the economy. There's nothing unexpected in saying that you're taking care of job online is the genuine pattern today. Indeed, most of side hustles today are done online with individuals utilizing their workstations and cell phones to acquire in their extra time. The main motivation why online side hustles are so well known is a direct result of its openness. Working on the web gives you the opportunity to work anyplace on the planet with just a PC and a web association for other people, they appreciate acquiring a nice measure of additional pay. All in the solaces of their own homes. Online gigs are advantageous for individuals with furious timetables, for example, guardians and shift laborers. Obviously, this isn't for everyone. Assuming your regular occupation as of now includes a huge load of online work, you'll just discover this twice as a weight to manage.

We should investigate the most well-known online side hustles out there and see what sort of additional chances are available for you. Outsourcing alludes to managing responsibilities for an assortment of customers. Typically, through low maintenance occupations or undertakings. Outsourcing work is typically dependent upon the situation and settled upon through agreements. Outsourcing is an incredible alternative for talented people who would prefer not to dedicate an enormous chunk of time to their side hustles to date. There are 1.1 billion online specialists all throughout the planet with 75% saying they wouldn't exchange it for other work. There are many outsourcing locales, for example, Upwork and Fiverr that posts a large number of undertakings. Consistently. Individuals enrolled on the stage can essentially pick a venture that coordinates with their abilities wanted rate, just as their own timetables. The most popular abilities are video altering, programming, visual computerization, composing, and bookkeeping or accounting.

Then again, there is additionally work that includes fewer specific abilities, however more authoritative capacities. This incorporates occupations like venture the board and being a remote helper, showing English, instructing English. Is anything but another idea. Many individuals became English mentors for youngsters or went abroad to educate outsiders. Be that as it may, as of late, internet instructing has gotten staggeringly well known in a few non-English talking nations, especially in Asia. As many individuals there are searching for approaches to learn English consistently, a great many individuals are searching for coaches to show them English. So, openings in this space are boundless. There are a great deal of organizations and stages that you can participate as an English educator. Having a few choices likewise permits you to pick what nation and segment you can discover understudies at. Notwithstanding, to acquire a higher rate, it is ideal to turn into a T E F L confirmed instructor first T E F L, or showing English as an unknown dialect is a universally perceived field for instructing English that gives proficient freedoms overall T E F L authorize educators procure more.

Regardless of whether in physical or virtual educating to get TFL confirmed, you can either take an expert course, a far-off based preparing or get affirmed abroad. Online overviews. Input is the fundamental factor for making upgrades. This is the reason organizations reward individuals who take as much time as necessary to give remarks and give ideas about their client encounters, this side hustle. Nonetheless, isn't the sort that can help you cover your bills, yet rather it's for those one, make some additional money in their leisure time. A few rewards additionally come as vouchers and limits. So, in case you're somebody who's searching for approaches to save in your next buy, then, at that point this present one's for you. Online overviews should be possible while you're unwinding, holding up in line or voyaging. Make a point to do your exploration first to discover a genuine site as summer simply tricks, that will just burn through your time.

Module Three

OK, welcome to module three. Furthermore, this module, our master will show you some disconnected side hustle alternatives. So, prepare to take a few notes and we should hop directly in

Module three disconnected side hustle thoughts. On the off chance that you don't view yourself as an educated individual, there are as two or three side hustles that you can do inside your compass. These sorts of occupations are useful to acquire educational experience and become more. As an individual disconnected side hustles are extraordinary for assisting your neighborhood local area. Being associated with such exercises likewise adds to better emotional well-being, as it gives you more motivation to remain dynamic and social disconnected side hustles include active work. However, assuming you appreciate circumventing town and meeting many individuals, this one suits you well. Ordinarily disconnected side hustles are typically secured through position openings or references. Nonetheless, a great deal of these are presently found on the web. You will not be straightforwardly utilizing the applications to bring in cash, yet it fills in as a device to help you look for some kind of employment with a basic bit of a catch.

You can participate in positions that give true encounters. Here are the absolute most well-known side hustles you can do disconnected ride share administration. On the off chance that you have a vehicle, you can bring in cash by enrolling for a ride sharing help like Uber or Lyft by basically turning into an independent cabbie. You can bring in cash by essentially cruising through the neighborhood. Fundamentally you work utilizing a versatile application that informs you. On the off chance that you have ride demands, it, the explores you to where to get and drop off traveler's ride share drivers have adaptable choices for you can work as per your timetable. This implies that you can reject rides or just pick clients that have a similar objective get-together off you're naturally paid through the application and may even get tips from liberal travelers' rates likewise change during times of heavy traffic. So, working during active times can assist you with procuring food conveyance.

While regarding the matter of driving, you can likewise utilize your driving abilities by joining a food conveyance administration like entryway run and grub center to apply all you need is a driver's permit with a perfect record and to telephone to utilize their application. A portion of these organizations additionally once in a while offer administrations utilizing cyclists. So, assuming you're searching for approaches to bring in cash while getting sufficient exercise, this presents one's for you leasing a space. On the off chance that you have an unused space, for example, an extra room or a subsequent home enlisting with online get-away rental organizations like Airbnb and VRBO is an extraordinary method to bring in some cash by just allowing others to utilize your space that in any case is left assembling. Just fundamentally you have your own space and give straightforward conveniences to travelers or for individuals visiting your region. No doubt. This side hustle is extraordinary for meeting new individuals and making new companions from various nations.

In any case, bring up that assuming you're the sort of individual who approaches their security in a serious way, this probably won't be the gig for you. In case you're hoping to lease your room, you should open your home to everyone by allowing total aliens to remain at your home. You comprehend that you need to make certain changes and may confront certain dangers and difficulties in managing them. These online excursion rental organizations had their portable application where you can list your space, give your ideal rate each night, your timetable, just as carrying out rules and conditions. When leasing your property, you can bring in a decent measure of cash with a side hustle, particularly on the off chance that you change your space into turning out to be cozier and making yourself a more cordial host. Another advantage of having the side hustle is that you can allocate others to routinely tidy up and keep up with your room or to go about as your cohost.

This gives you the choice to turn out to be less included and transform it into an automated revenue. What are you hanging tight for Jordan side hustling labor force and procure the extra a hundred dollars every month, regardless of whether it's using your abilities and gifts, supporting your nearby local area, or just accomplishing something in your available energy will certainly engage you realizing that you can keep on flourishing? Notwithstanding the difficulties that we manage each day, this side hustling world is simply on the opposite side. You should simply go out on a limb really at that time truly you encountered the unlimited chances the world has to bring to the table.

Don't miss out!

Visit the website below and you can sign up to receive emails whenever B. Vincent publishes a new book. There's no charge and no obligation.

https://books2read.com/r/B-A-QWUO-TEFRB

BOOKS 2 READ

Connecting independent readers to independent writers.

Also by B. Vincent

Bookkeeping
Bridge Pages
Business Acquisition
Business Bogging
Marketing Automation
Better Meetings
Conversion Optimization
Creative Solutions
Employee Recruitment
Startup Capital
Employee Mentoring
Followership
Servant Leadership
Human Resources
Team Building
Freelancing
Funnel Building
Geo Targeting
Goal Setting
Immanent List Building
Lead Generation
Leadership Course
Leadership Transition
LinkedIn Ads
LinkedIn Marketing
Messenger Marketing
New Management
Newsfeed Ads
Search Ads
Online Learning
Sales Webinars

Side Hustles

About the Publisher

Accepting manuscripts in the most categories. We love to help people get their words available to the world.

Revival Waves of Glory focus is to provide more options to be published. We do traditional paperbacks, hardcovers, audio books and ebooks all over the world. A traditional royalty-based publisher that offers self-publishing options, Revival Waves provides a very author friendly and transparent publishing process, with President Bill Vincent involved in the full process of your book. Send us your manuscript and we will contact you as soon as possible.

Contact: Bill Vincent at rwgpublishing@yahoo.com www.rwgpublishing.com